HOW TO DRAW CARS

**Illustrated by
Karen Ann McKee**

**MALLARD
PRESS**

An Imprint of BDD Promotional Book Company, Inc.
666 Fifth Avenue
New York, N.Y. 10103

Mallard Press and its accompanying design and logo
are trademarks of BDD Promotional Book Company, Inc.

First published in the United States of America
in 1991 by The Mallard Press
ISBN 0-7924-5571-1

Introduction

This book will show you some easy ways to draw lots of different cars. Some may be more difficult than others, but if you follow along, step-by-step, you'll soon be able to draw any car you wish.

Using the basic shapes illustrated below will help you get started. Remember that these shapes, in different sizes and combinations, will change from car to car. Variations of these shapes will also be used. Refer, too, to the terms listed. They will help you refine and complete your pictures.

CIRCLE

A **Circle** is a perfectly round shape.

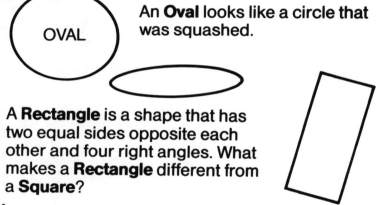

OVAL

An **Oval** looks like a circle that was squashed.

A **Square** is a shape that has four equal sides and four right angles.

SQUARE

A **Rectangle** is a shape that has two equal sides opposite each other and four right angles. What makes a **Rectangle** different from a **Square**?

RECTANGLE

A **Triangle** is a shape that has three angles and three sides.

TRIANGLE

DIAMOND

A **Diamond** shape is made by putting two **Triangles** together at their bases.

A **Wedge** shape is tapered at one end to look like a "V."

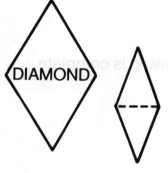

WEDGE

SUPPLIES

NUMBER 2 PENCILS
SOFT ERASER
DRAWING PAD

FELT-TIP PENS (thick and thin points)
COLORED PENCILS, MARKERS, OR CRAYONS

Front side view

Other important terms:

DIMENSION   Objects have three dimensions: width, height, and depth.

VIEWPOINT is the position from which you see an object. Examples: top view, side view, rear view; or a combination like front side view.

PERSPECTIVE   When you show an object's three dimensions, you are showing it in perspective and from a viewpoint.

CONTOUR   The shape of an object or its outline.

OVERLAP   To cover one part of an object with part of another object.

BUTT   Joining objects end to end, but not overlapping them.

Side view

Head-on

Rear side view

Helpful Hints

Before starting your first drawing, you may want to practice tracing the different steps. Start your drawing by lightly sketching out the first step. The first step is very important and should be done carefully. The second step will be sketched over the first one. Next, refine and blend the shapes together, erasing any guidelines you no longer need. Add final details. When your drawing is complete, go over your pencil lines with a felt-tip pen. You might want to draw a thicker line for the outer shape of your car and a thinner line for the contours and details. If you wish,

you may color your drawing with markers, pencils, or crayons.

Each car has special characteristics that make it easier or, in some cases, more difficult to draw. However, it's easy to draw anything when you break it down into simple shapes! Remember, practice makes perfect, so keep drawing until you've mastered each car. Use your imagination. Add drivers, roads, backgrounds; create a scene with two or more cars; and most of all, HAVE FUN!

Parts of a Car

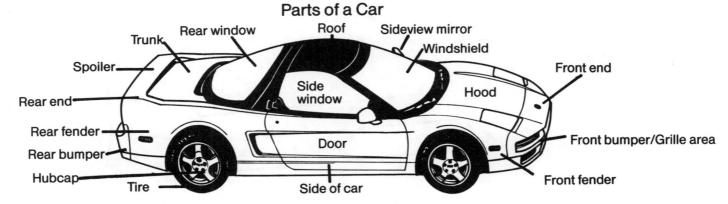

1985 Lamborghini Countach

This hot car has been making gut-wrenching getaways since its introduction in 1971. The Countach zooms from 0-60 in 5.9 seconds. Collectible models sell easily for $100,000 to upwards of $200,000!

1. Start with a large 4-sided shape to form the hood and one side of the car. Add a rectangular shape for the front bumper, and finish the side panel with lines that form a wedge, as shown. Then draw two oval guidelines for each visible tire.

Note: It is always easier to draw the largest shape first, then add the smaller shapes.

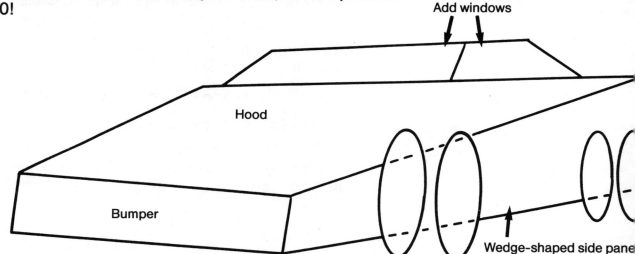

Add windows

Hood

Bumper

Wedge-shaped side panel

2. Next, add three curved lines to shape the hood of the car. Then connect each pair of ovals to form the tires. Draw a line to divide the front bumper area in half and continue this line around the front end to the wheel.

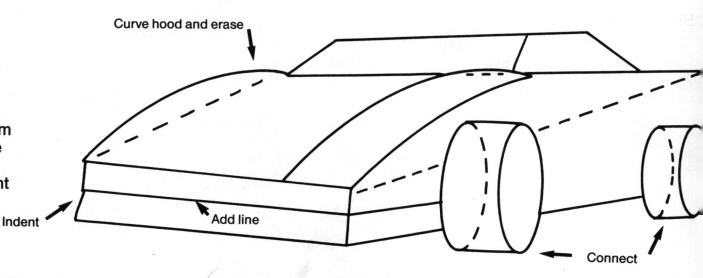

Curve hood and erase

Indent

Add line

Connect

Add lines and rectangles on the hood and bumper, as shown. Shape around the tires and erase the guidelines. Add lines for the window frame, door, and the spoiler at the rear.

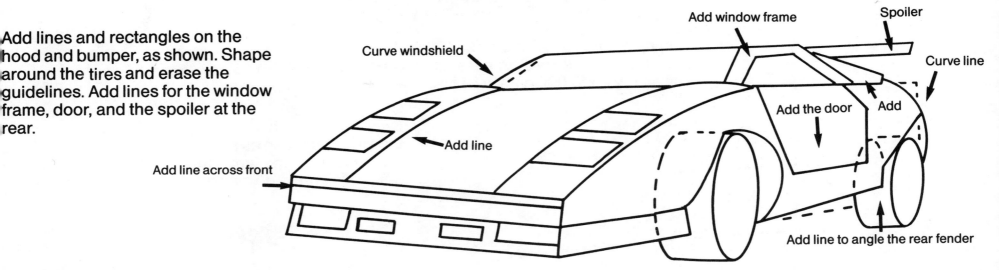

Curve windshield

Add window frame

Spoiler

Curve line

Add the door

Add

Add line

Add line across front

Add line to angle the rear fender

Hint: Draw the basic shapes lightly. These guidelines will be erased later.

Blend all lines to give the car a smooth, sleek look. Add final details and shading. A sideview mirror, door handle, and hubcaps complete this supercar!

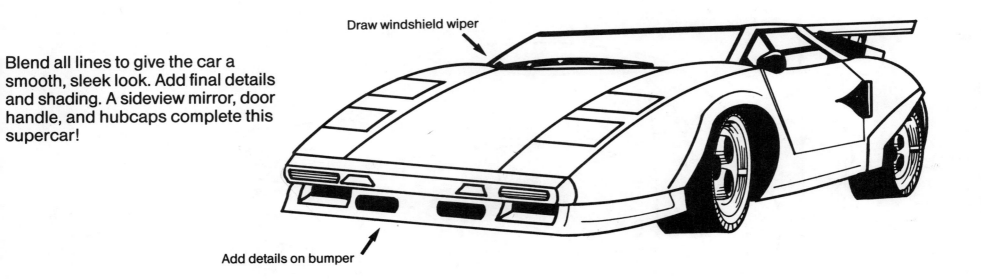

Draw windshield wiper

Add details on bumper

1964 Mustang

Originally introduced at the 1964 World's Fair in New York, the Mustang was Ford's most successful model of the day— selling over 600,000 cars in its first year!

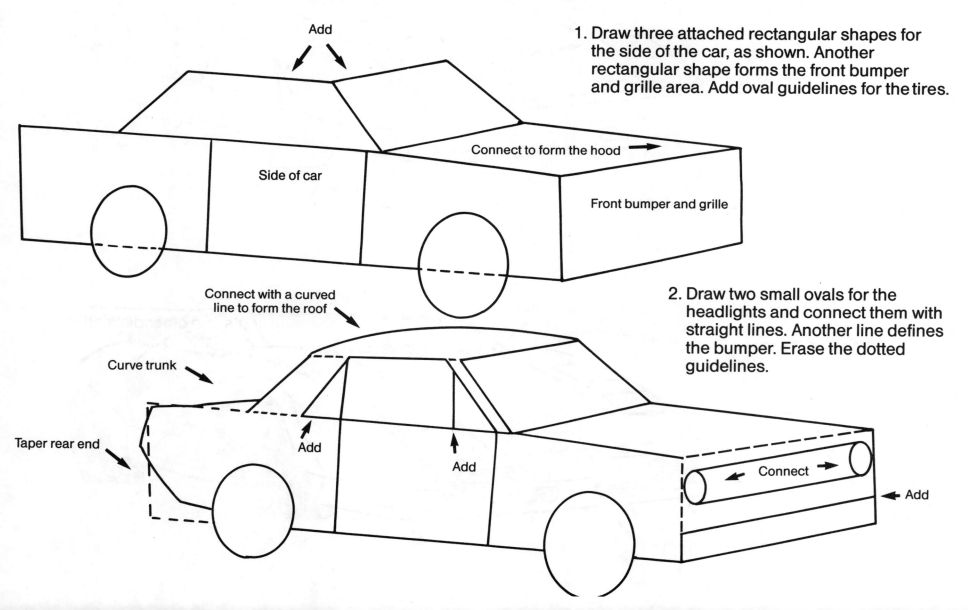

Add

1. Draw three attached rectangular shapes for the side of the car, as shown. Another rectangular shape forms the front bumper and grille area. Add oval guidelines for the tires.

Connect to form the hood →

Side of car

Front bumper and grille

Connect with a curved line to form the roof

2. Draw two small ovals for the headlights and connect them with straight lines. Another line defines the bumper. Erase the dotted guidelines.

Curve trunk

Taper rear end

Add

Add

← Connect →

← Add

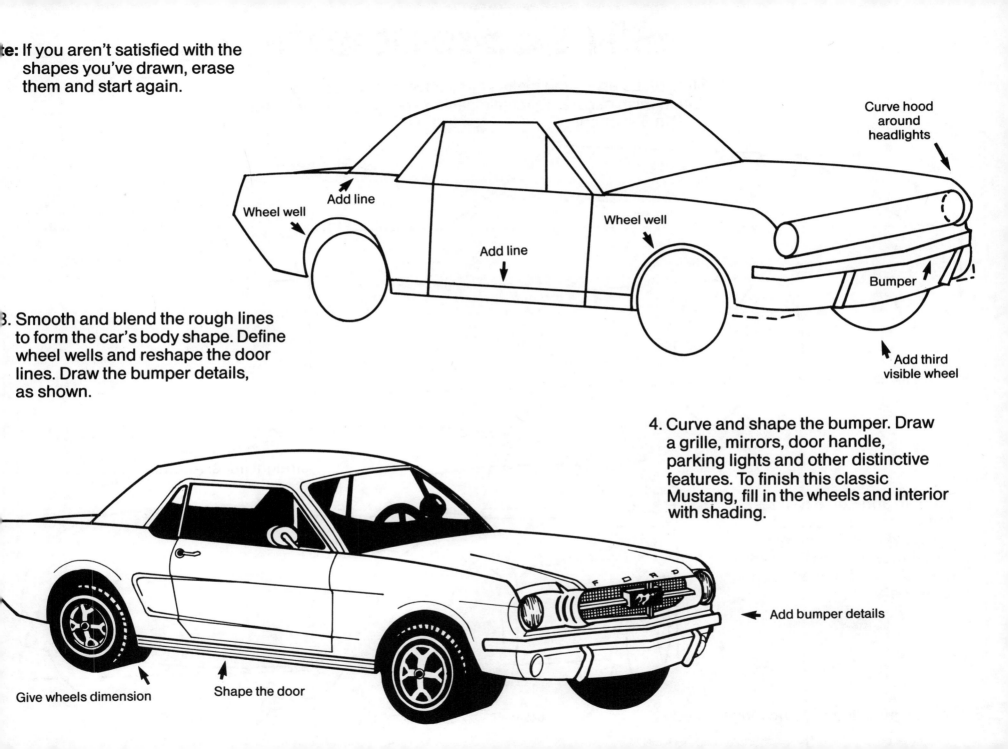

te: If you aren't satisfied with the shapes you've drawn, erase them and start again.

Curve hood around headlights

Add line

Wheel well

Add line

Wheel well

Bumper

Add third visible wheel

3. Smooth and blend the rough lines to form the car's body shape. Define wheel wells and reshape the door lines. Draw the bumper details, as shown.

4. Curve and shape the bumper. Draw a grille, mirrors, door handle, parking lights and other distinctive features. To finish this classic Mustang, fill in the wheels and interior with shading.

Add bumper details

Give wheels dimension

Shape the door

1991 Dodge Stealth

State of the art styling makes this subcompact Dodge a dream-wish car. Aerodynamic design speeds the Stealth from 0-60 in 6 seconds.

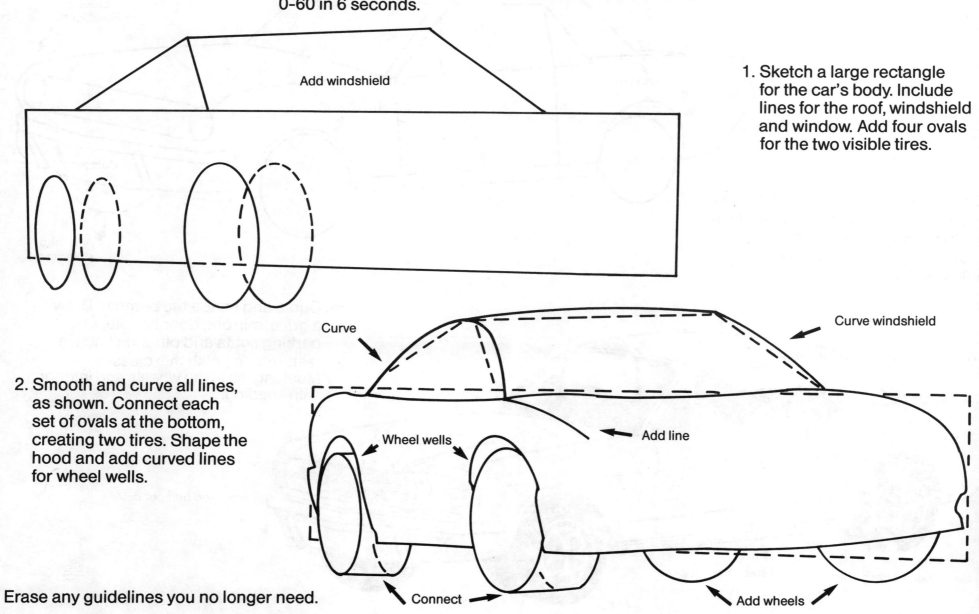

Add windshield

1. Sketch a large rectangle for the car's body. Include lines for the roof, windshield and window. Add four ovals for the two visible tires.

Curve

Curve windshield

2. Smooth and curve all lines, as shown. Connect each set of ovals at the bottom, creating two tires. Shape the hood and add curved lines for wheel wells.

Wheel wells

Add line

Erase any guidelines you no longer need.

Connect

Add wheels

Window frame

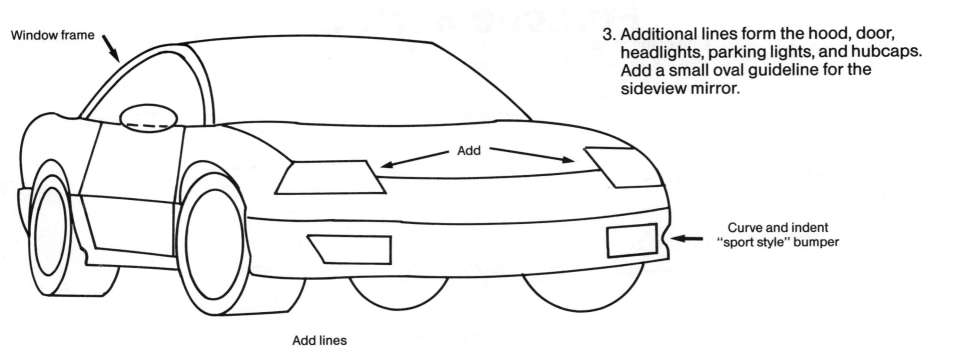

3. Additional lines form the hood, door, headlights, parking lights, and hubcaps. Add a small oval guideline for the sideview mirror.

Add

Curve and indent "sport style" bumper

Add lines to create small window

Draw the final details carefully. Use markers to fill in the shading on the roof, bumper details, tires and hubcaps.

nt: For a more dramatic effect, use a thicker pen or marker for the outer shape of the car and a thin marker or pen for the inner contour lines.

Porsche 917/30

One of the most powerful sports cars ever built, this Porsche was the 1973 Can Am Champion.

Note: Be sure to extend wedge shape past top of car.

1. To draw the top and side, start with the two large shapes. Then, complete the small rectangular shape for the front bumper. Now, add other basic shapes as shown.

Rectangular shape forms top of car

Add triangle

Overlaps hood and bumper

Wedge for side

Add triangle

Front bumper

2. Next, draw two long, flowing, curved lines from the rear fins to the front fenders. Then, add lines to form the spoiler, as shown.

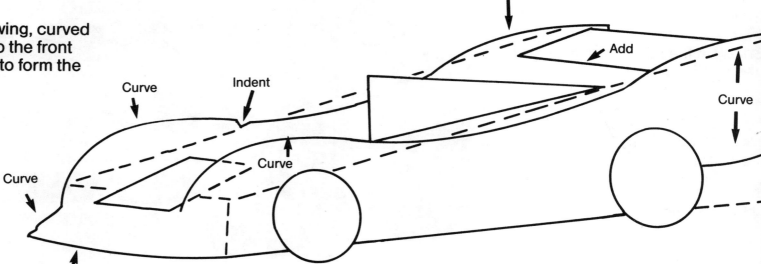

Curve

Add

Curve

Indent

Curve

Curve

Curve

Curve

Note: Take your time. If necessary, erase and start again.

Add contour lines to the front fenders. Draw a cylinder on the front of the car, as shown. Next, shape the wheel wells. Then, position an oval for the racer's helmet, and behind it, a wedge for the headrest.

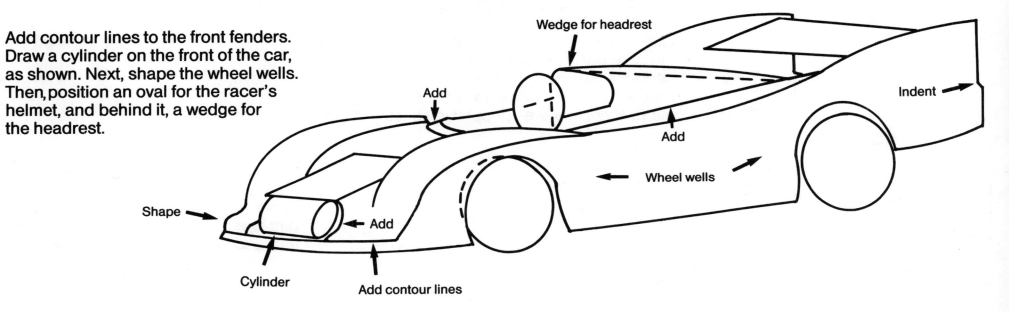

Wedge for headrest

Add

Indent

Add

Shape

Cylinder

Add

Add contour lines

Wheel wells

Complete this "raging rider" with vents, wheels, decals, mirrors and other details. Shade in the racer's helmet—and you're off.

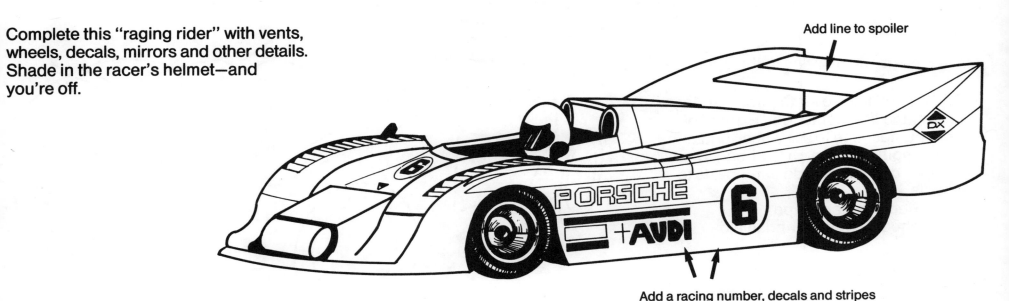

Add line to spoiler

PORSCHE

+AUDI

6

DX

Add a racing number, decals and stripes

1977 Corvette Stingray

Often referred to as the all-American sports car, the Stingray is low-slung and slant-nosed for high performance and excellent handling. The 500,000th production 'Vette was sold in 1977 showing the durability of this ever-popular, distinctive design.

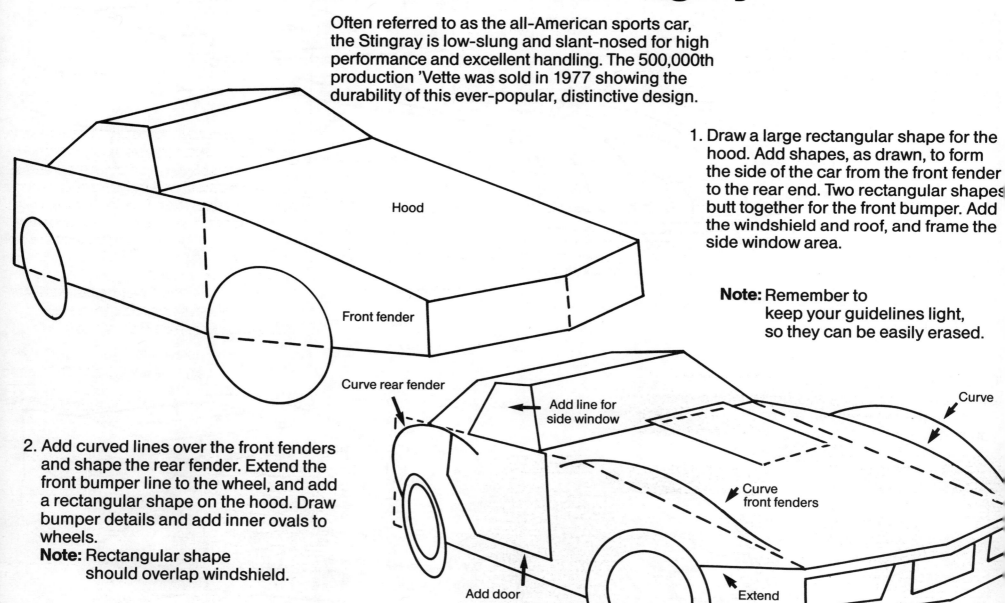

1. Draw a large rectangular shape for the hood. Add shapes, as drawn, to form the side of the car from the front fender to the rear end. Two rectangular shapes butt together for the front bumper. Add the windshield and roof, and frame the side window area.

Note: Remember to keep your guidelines light, so they can be easily erased.

2. Add curved lines over the front fenders and shape the rear fender. Extend the front bumper line to the wheel, and add a rectangular shape on the hood. Draw bumper details and add inner ovals to wheels.
Note: Rectangular shape should overlap windshield.

Hood

Front fender

Curve rear fender

Add line for side window

Curve

Curve front fenders

Add door

Extend

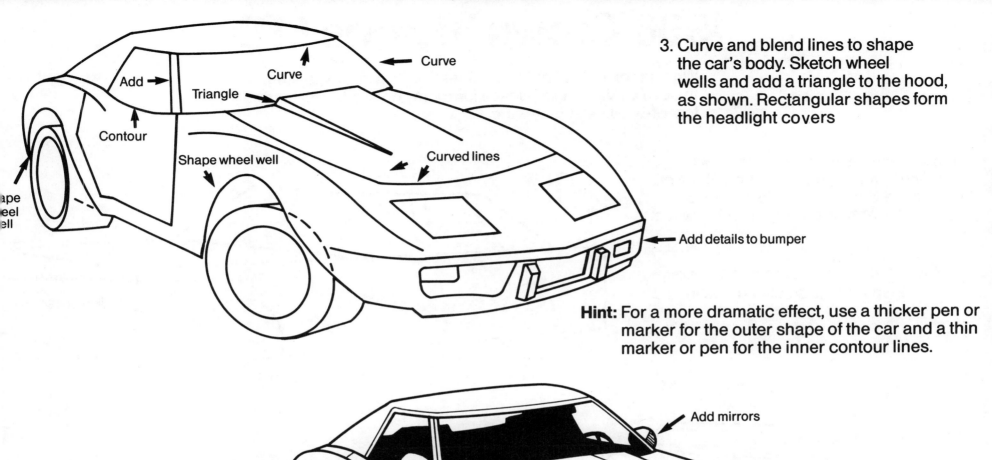

Curve

Add

Curve

Triangle

Contour

Shape wheel well

Shape wheel well

Curved lines

Add details to bumper

3. Curve and blend lines to shape the car's body. Sketch wheel wells and add a triangle to the hood, as shown. Rectangular shapes form the headlight covers

Hint: For a more dramatic effect, use a thicker pen or marker for the outer shape of the car and a thin marker or pen for the inner contour lines.

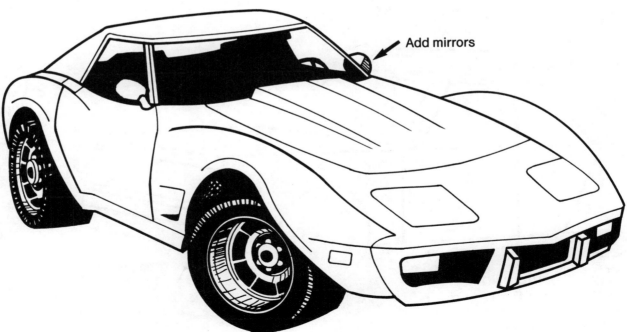

Add mirrors

Complete the Stingray by adding mirrors and other details. Add final touches by shading the interior, wheels and bumper.

1990 Crown Victoria LTD

Whether on official police business or day-to-day driving, the Crown Vic is a showcase for roomy comfortability and top-of-the-line engineering.

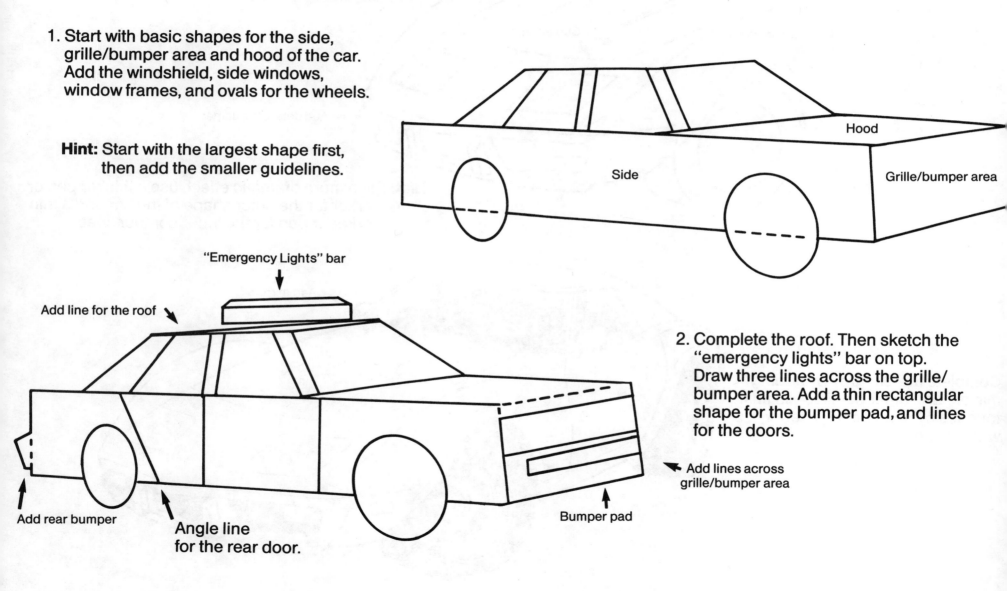

1. Start with basic shapes for the side, grille/bumper area and hood of the car. Add the windshield, side windows, window frames, and ovals for the wheels.

   Hint: Start with the largest shape first, then add the smaller guidelines.

Hood

Side

Grille/bumper area

"Emergency Lights" bar

Add line for the roof

2. Complete the roof. Then sketch the "emergency lights" bar on top. Draw three lines across the grille/bumper area. Add a thin rectangular shape for the bumper pad, and lines for the doors.

Add lines across grille/bumper area

Add rear bumper

Angle line for the rear door.

Bumper pad

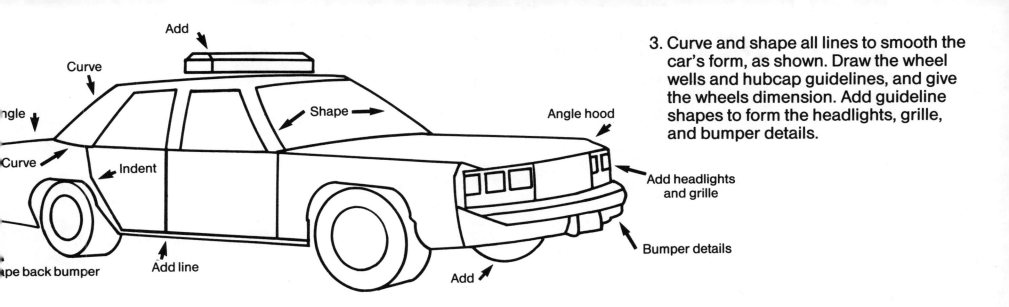

Add

Curve

ngle

Curve

Indent

Shape →

Angle hood

Add headlights
and grille

Bumper details

pe back bumper

Add line

Add ↗

3. Curve and shape all lines to smooth the car's form, as shown. Draw the wheel wells and hubcap guidelines, and give the wheels dimension. Add guideline shapes to form the headlights, grille, and bumper details.

4. Shade the roof, hood and wheels. Add trim around the windows, and draw the siren and mirror, as shown. For the finishing touches add door handles, emblem, vehicle number, and front-end details.

For effect, add sound and light accents and, suddenly, you're in hot pursuit!

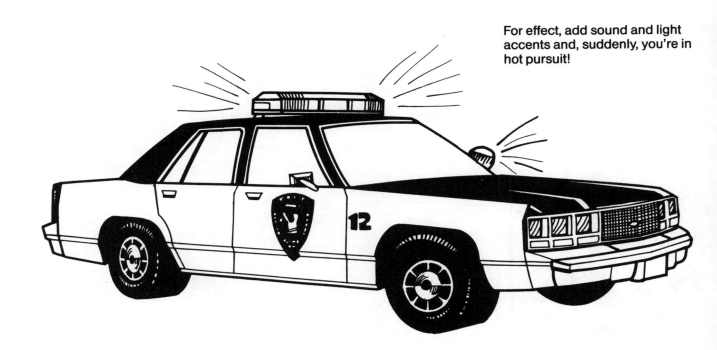

1991 Lotus Turbo Esprit SE

This outstanding import goes from 0-60 in a head-spinning
5.1 seconds! The Lotus reaches maximum speed of 165mph.
Its 280 horsepower drives this quick-as-lightning car!

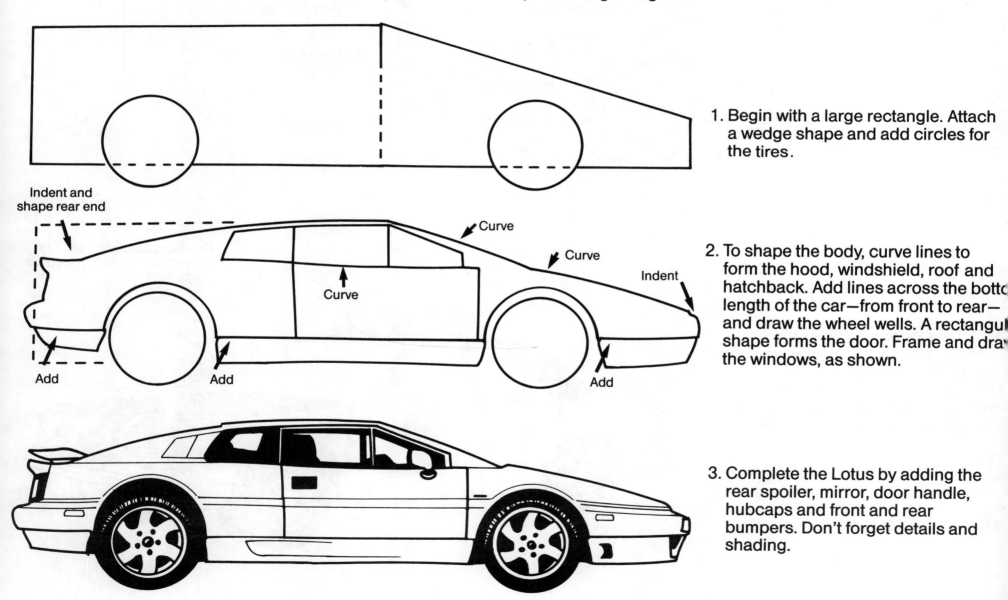

1. Begin with a large rectangle. Attach a wedge shape and add circles for the tires.

2. To shape the body, curve lines to form the hood, windshield, roof and hatchback. Add lines across the botto length of the car—from front to rear— and draw the wheel wells. A rectangu shape forms the door. Frame and dra the windows, as shown.

3. Complete the Lotus by adding the rear spoiler, mirror, door handle, hubcaps and front and rear bumpers. Don't forget details and shading.

1991 Chevy Camaro Z28

Coupe or convertible, the Camaro's windswept
curves will carry you to adventure.

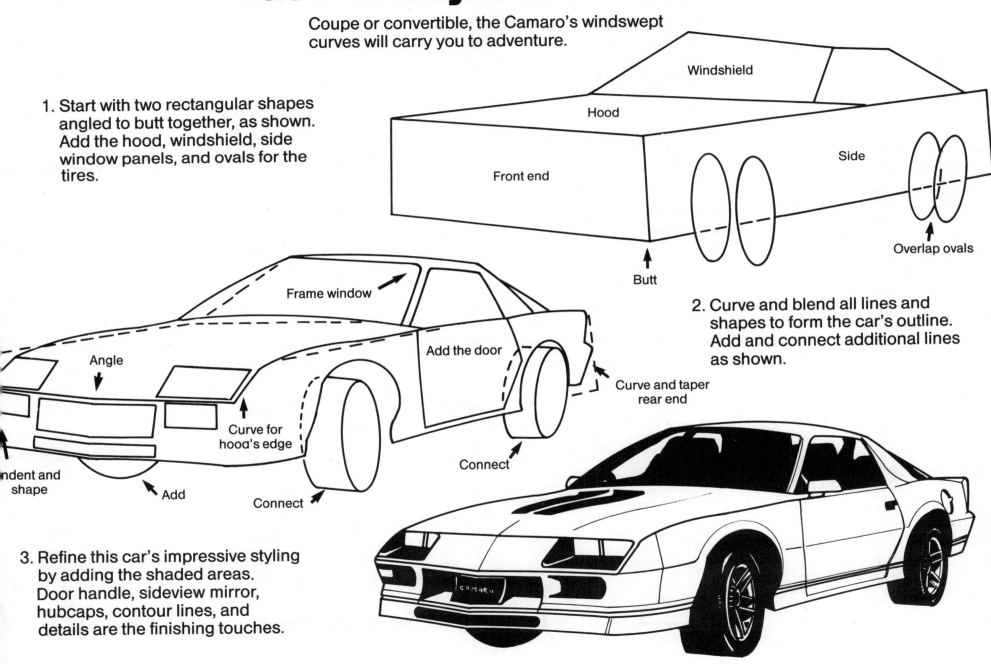

1. Start with two rectangular shapes
   angled to butt together, as shown.
   Add the hood, windshield, side
   window panels, and ovals for the
   tires.

Windshield

Hood

Front end

Side

Overlap ovals

Butt

Frame window

Angle

Add the door

Curve and taper
rear end

Curve for
hood's edge

Connect

ndent and
shape

Add

Connect

2. Curve and blend all lines and
   shapes to form the car's outline.
   Add and connect additional lines
   as shown.

3. Refine this car's impressive styling
   by adding the shaded areas.
   Door handle, sideview mirror,
   hubcaps, contour lines, and
   details are the finishing touches.

CAMARO

1991 Acura NSX

The world's first all aluminum car! In a class by itself, this car's design was inspired by the F-16 jet aircraft. With a top speed of 168mph, driven by 270 horsepower, this light - weight car is no lightweight! Goes from 0-60 in 5.5 seconds.

1. Begin with a large rectangular shape butted to a wedge shape, as shown. Draw a large oval to form the roof, windshield, and windows. Add ovals for the wheels and complete the front end area.

2. Draw lines for the windows, door, and headlights. Add a small rectangle for the rear bumper.

← Add

Rectangle

← Angle line

Curve and shape the out-
line of the car. Smooth hood
lines, and contour rear and
front bumpers.

ote Styling the spoiler is
tricky! Take your time
to get it right. If you're
not satisfied with the
lines or shapes you've
drawn, erase them
and start again.

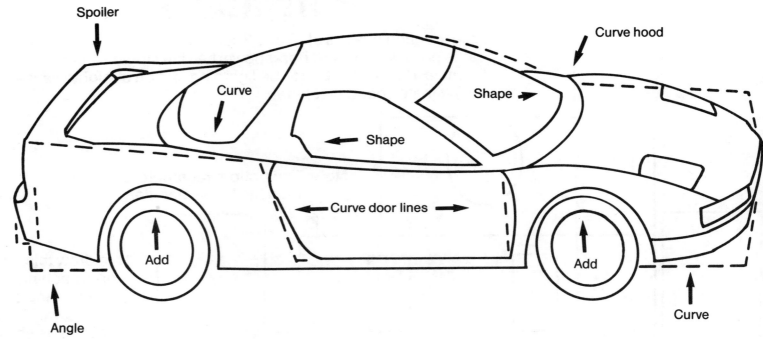

Spoiler

Curve hood

Curve

Shape

Shape

Contour bumper

Curve door lines

Add

Add

Angle

Curve

Add lines to refine the
windows and roof as you
shade-in details. Curved
contour lines, mirrors, hubcap details and windshield
wipers complete this high-
performance road master.

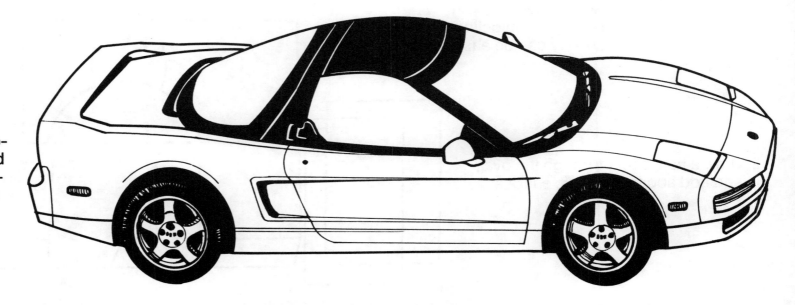

Formula 1

Able to reach speeds of nearly 200mph, the Formula 1 racing car is propelled by 450 horsepower! A slim single seater, Formula 1's are stripped to be lightning fast on straightaways—the ultimate speed machine!

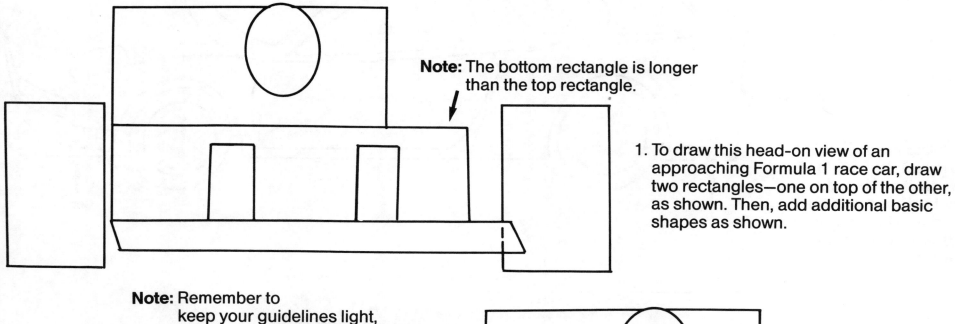

Note: The bottom rectangle is longer than the top rectangle.

1. To draw this head-on view of an approaching Formula 1 race car, draw two rectangles—one on top of the other, as shown. Then, add additional basic shapes as shown.

Note: Remember to keep your guidelines light, so they can be easily erased.

2. Draw a half-circle through the oval, and add additional basic shapes.

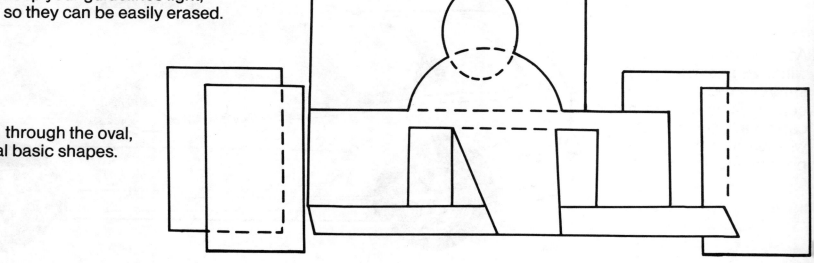

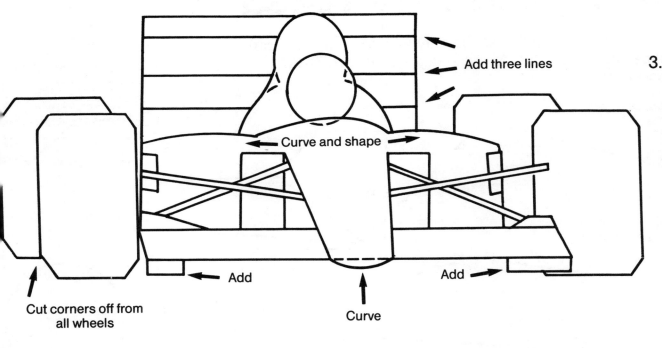

Add three lines

Curve and shape

Add

Add

Cut corners off from
all wheels

Curve

3. Add crossed bars from the tires to
the nose of the car. Curve the tip of
the car's nose and add a circle at
the top. Curve and shape the driver's
cockpit. Add additional shapes,
as shown.

4. Add lots of shading and details to
complete the Formula 1. Draw the
driver's helmet, mirrors, a racing
number and insignia to identify this
mighty master of the raceway!

1991 Ferrari Testarossa

Short on height—the Testarossa is only 44.5 inches high—but high on performance, this driving delight goes form 0-60 in 6.2 seconds.

1. Start by drawing three attached rectangular shapes to form the side of the car. Add other shapes for the front bumper, hood, windshield, roof, and hatch-back. Add circles for the tires and lines for the door.

Remember to keep your guidelines light.

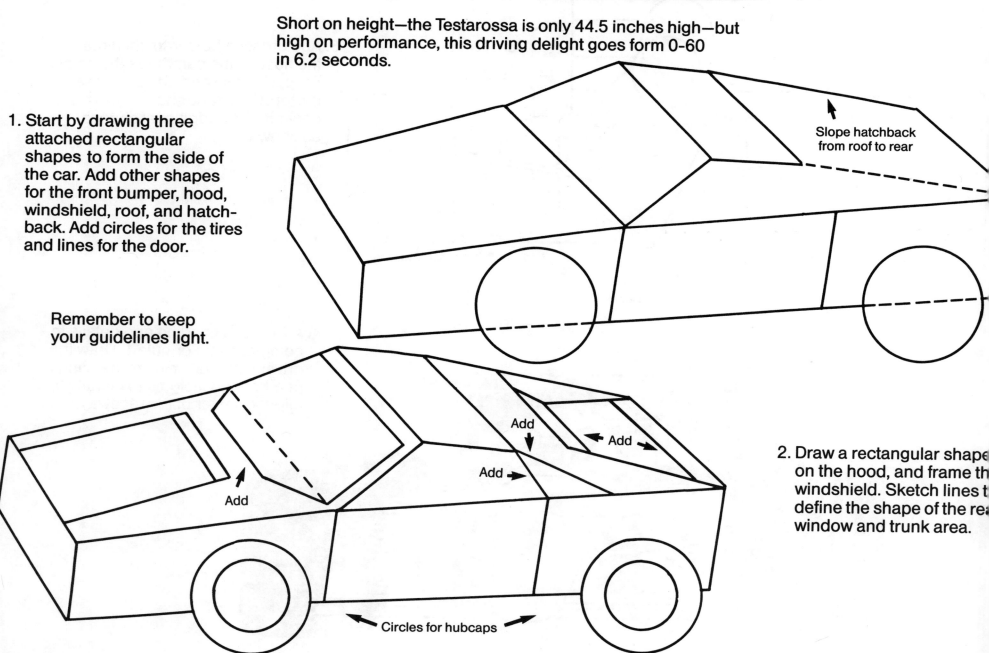

Slope hatchback from roof to rear

Add

Add

Add

Add

Circles for hubcaps

2. Draw a rectangular shape on the hood, and frame th windshield. Sketch lines t define the shape of the re window and trunk area.

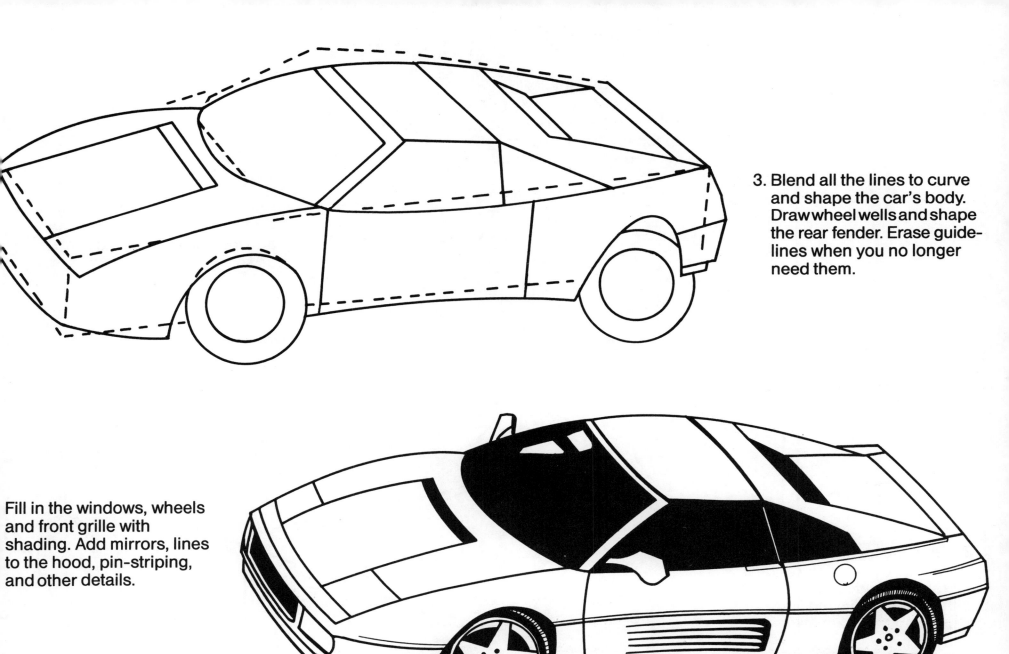

3. Blend all the lines to curve
and shape the car's body.
Draw wheel wells and shape
the rear fender. Erase guidelines when you no longer
need them.

Fill in the windows, wheels
and front grille with
shading. Add mirrors, lines
to the hood, pin-striping,
and other details.

1991 Nissan 300 ZX

An easy-to-handle, subcompact two-seater with flawless styling makes the Nissan a comfortable neighborhood cruiser or a hard-to-catch sports car. Reaches a top speed of 148mph and goes from 0-60 in 7.1 seconds.

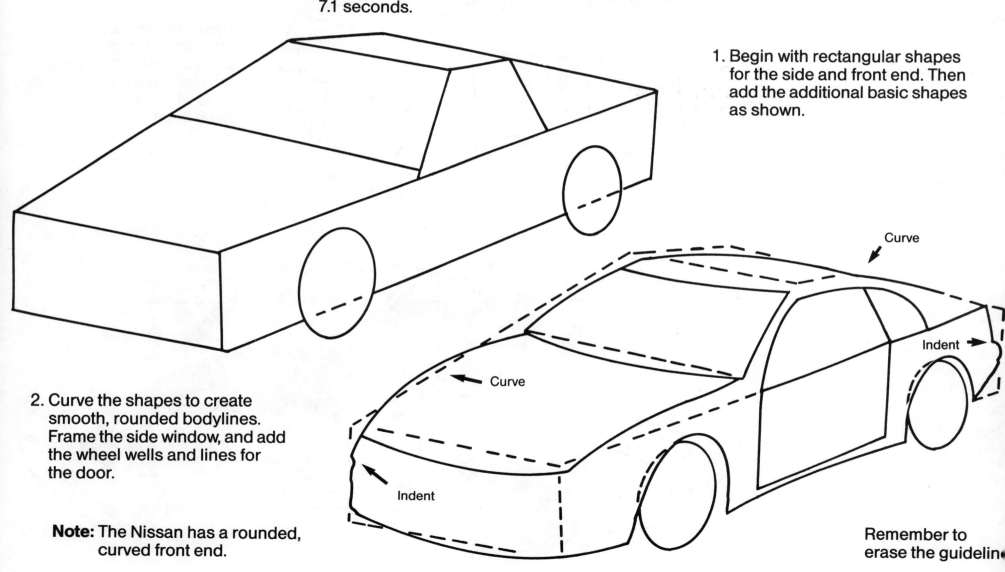

1. Begin with rectangular shapes for the side and front end. Then add the additional basic shapes as shown.

Curve

Curve

Indent

2. Curve the shapes to create smooth, rounded bodylines. Frame the side window, and add the wheel wells and lines for the door.

Indent

Note: The Nissan has a rounded, curved front end.

Remember to erase the guidelines.

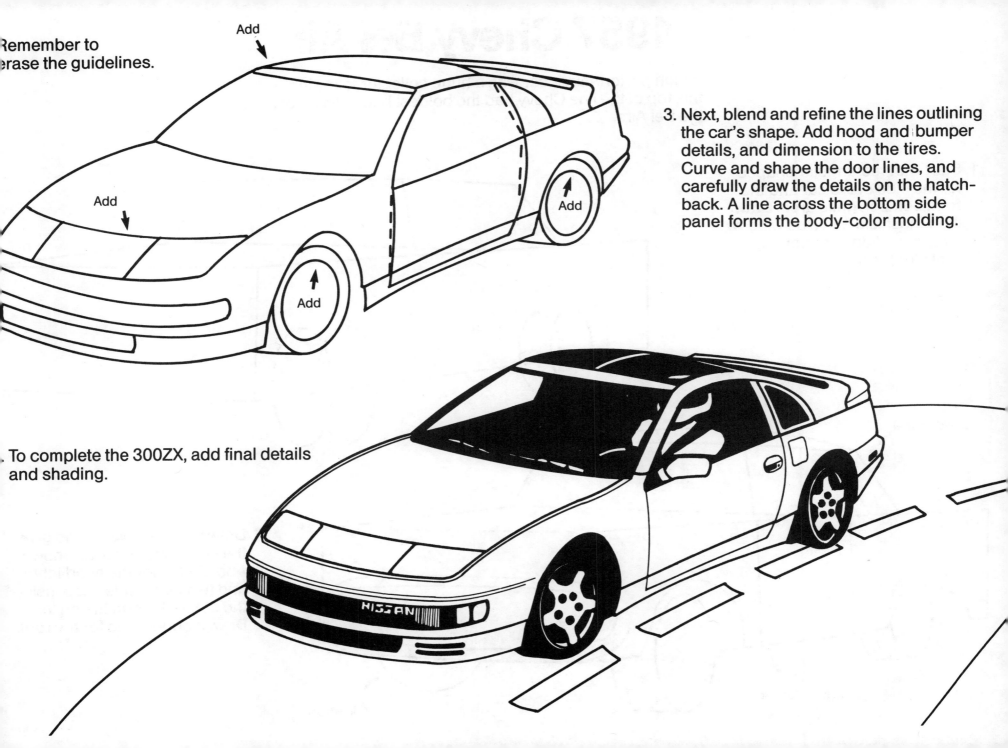

Remember to
erase the guidelines.

Add

Add

Add

Add

3. Next, blend and refine the lines outlining
the car's shape. Add hood and bumper
details, and dimension to the tires.
Curve and shape the door lines, and
carefully draw the details on the hatch-
back. A line across the bottom side
panel forms the body-color molding.

To complete the 300ZX, add final details
and shading.

NISSAN

1957 Chevy Bel Air

A high performance car with a huge collector following, this top of the line Chevy had the boldest body styling of all the Bel Airs.

1. Start with rectangular shapes for the side of the car and the front bumper/grille area. Draw the windshield and side window, as shown. Add overlapping ovals for the tires.

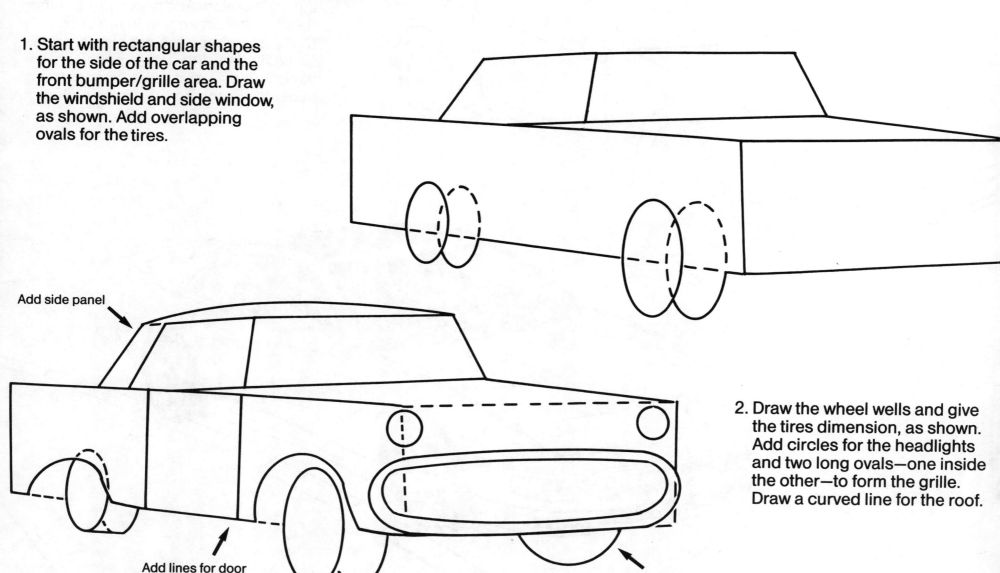

Add side panel

Add lines for door

Add wheel

2. Draw the wheel wells and give the tires dimension, as shown. Add circles for the headlights and two long ovals—one inside the other—to form the grille. Draw a curved line for the roof.

Shape the car's outline with curved lines. Add shapes around the headlights, as shown. Then begin drawing the grille/bumper details.

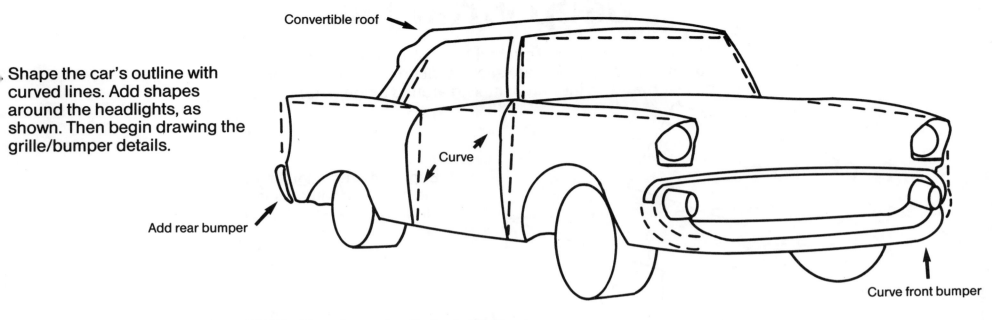

Convertible roof

Curve

Add rear bumper

Curve front bumper

Note: Erase and start again if you're not satisfied with the lines or shapes you've drawn.

4. Lastly, complete the grille and add side windows, hubcaps, door handle, and hood ornaments. Finish the Bell Air with body details and lots of shading.

Jeep Wrangler

An off-road vehicle that offers riders out-of-this-world adventure. Late models are seen as much on the main streets and highways as they are rambling around tough terrain.

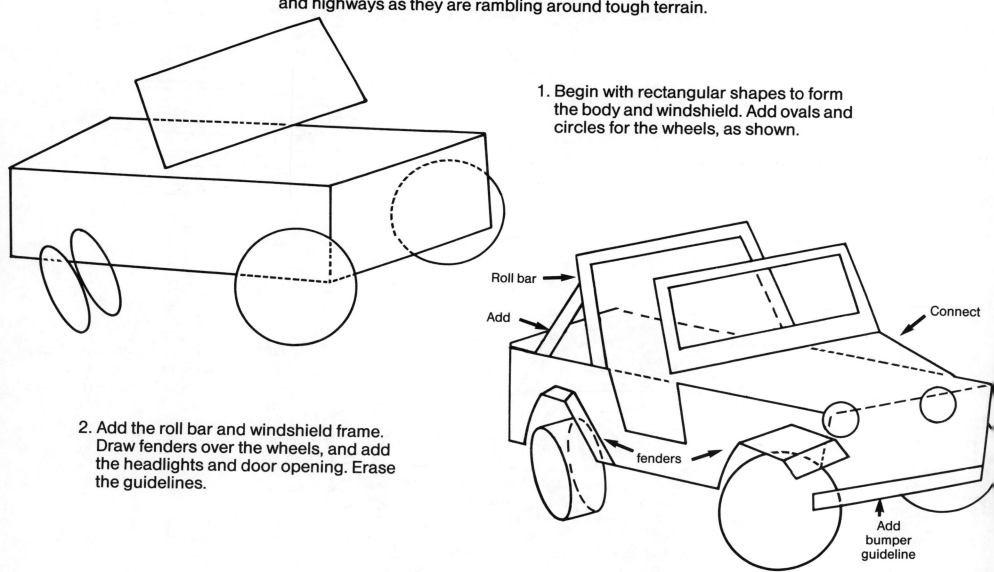

1. Begin with rectangular shapes to form the body and windshield. Add ovals and circles for the wheels, as shown.

Roll bar

Add

Connect

2. Add the roll bar and windshield frame. Draw fenders over the wheels, and add the headlights and door opening. Erase the guidelines.

fenders

Add bumper guideline

Note: It's easier to erase when your lines are lightly drawn.

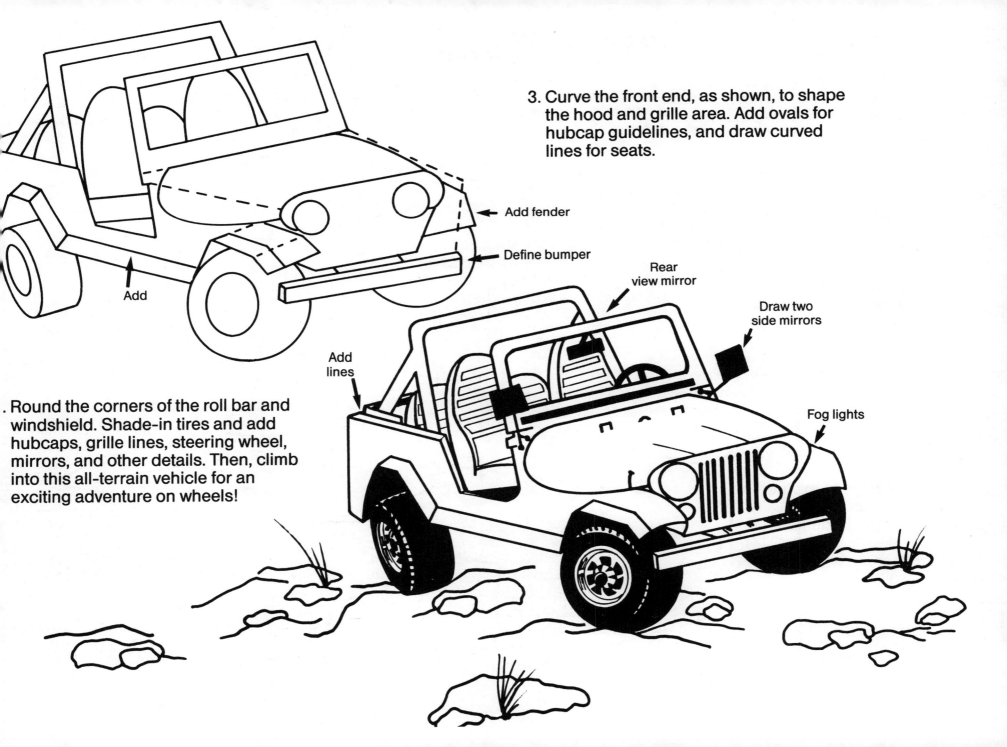

3. Curve the front end, as shown, to shape the hood and grille area. Add ovals for hubcap guidelines, and draw curved lines for seats.

Add fender

Define bumper

Add

Rear view mirror

Draw two side mirrors

Add lines

Fog lights

. Round the corners of the roll bar and windshield. Shade-in tires and add hubcaps, grille lines, steering wheel, mirrors, and other details. Then, climb into this all-terrain vehicle for an exciting adventure on wheels!

1955 Thunderbird

Take flight in this 2-door convertible and you'll know why the T-bird was one of the most sought after cars of its day. Its uncompromising styling set standards for years to come.

1. Draw a large, 3-dimensional rectangular shape, as shown, forming the car's body. Add lines for the door and extend them across the top. Draw ovals for the tires.

Rearview perspective

2. A wedge shape forms the special wraparound windshield—a trademark of this exciting car! Draw taillights, rear bumper and wheel wells.

Wraparound windshield

Taillights

Shape wheel wells

Shape and curve the car's outline. Add lines for the trunk and draw a circle to form the steering wheel. Add oval guidelines over the rear bumper and bumper details, as shown. Add dimension to the tires.

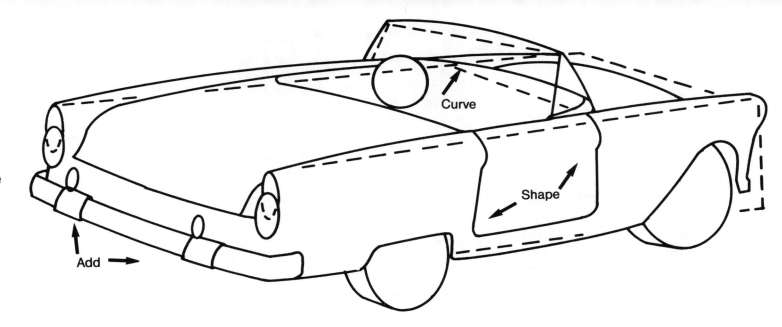

Curve

Shape

Add →

Remember: Erase and refine your lines as necessary.

To finish this classic Thunderbird, draw all the details including body contours and dashboard.

Thunderbird

1991 911 Porsche Turbo

With 50% more power added to the engine, the 911 reaches a top speed of 168mph and goes from 0-60 in 4.8 seconds!

1. Draw a large egg-shaped oval and a rectangle for the car's body. Add circles for the wheels and a diamond for the front bumper.

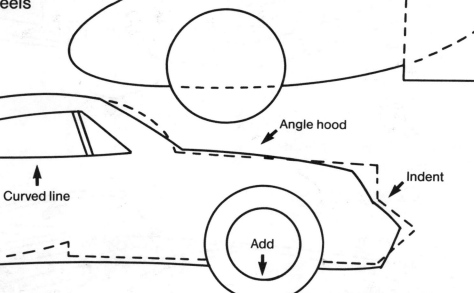

Angle hood

Indent

Curved line

Add

Add

2. Curve and blend the car's outline. Add the side windows and guidelines to separate each window.

3. Add the front and rear windshields. Add curved door lines and lines for the bumpers. Then, complete the hubcaps, and add final details and shading.

Add

Define rear bumper